SEATTLE SEAHAWKS

BY JOSH ANDERSON

Stride
An Imprint of The Child's World®
childsworld.com

Published by The Child's World®
800-599-READ • www.childsworld.com

Copyright © 2023 by The Child's World®
All rights reserved. No part of this book may be reproduced or utilized in any form of by any means without written permission from the publisher.

Photography Credits
Cover: © Steph Chambers / Staff / Getty Images; page 1: © Africa Studio / Shutterstock; page 3: © John Rivera/Icon Sportswire / Newscom; page 5: © Steve Dykes / Stringer / Getty Images; page 6: © George Rose / Stringer / Getty Images; page 9: © Harry How / Staff / Getty Images; page 10: © Otto Greule Jr / Stringer / Getty Images; page 11: © stevezmina1 / Getty Images; page 12: © Abbie Parr / Stringer / Getty Images; page 12: © Chris Unger / Stringer / Getty Images; page 13: © Kevin Casey / Stringer / Getty Images; page 13: © Lindsey Wasson / Stringer / Getty Images; page 14: © Christian Petersen / Staff / Getty Images; page 15: © Lawrence Iles/Icon Sportswire / Newscom; page 16: © Tom Hauck / Staff / Getty Images; page 16: © Tim DeFrisco / Stringer / Getty Images; page 17: © Brian Drake / SportsChrome / Newscom; page 17: © Elsa / Staff / Getty Images; page 18: © Vic Condiotty/MCT / Newscom; page 18: © Robert Giroux / Staff / Getty Images; page 19: © Otto Greule Jr / Stringer / Getty Images; page 19: © Kevin C. Cox / Staff / Getty Images; page 20: © Steph Chambers / Staff / Getty Images; page 20: © Steph Chambers / Staff / Getty Images; page 21: © David Berding / Stringer / Getty Images; page 21: © Stacy Revere / Staff / Getty Images; page 22: © Abbie Parr / Stringer / Getty Images; page 23: © Otto Greule Jr / Stringer / Getty Images; page 23: © stevezmina1 / Getty Images; page 25: © Rob Carr / Staff / Getty Images; page 26: © Michael Hickey / Stringer / Getty Images; page 29: © Otto Greule Jr / Stringer / Getty Images

ISBN Information
9781503857926 (Reinforced Library Binding)
9781503860667 (Portable Document Format)
9781503862029 (Online Multi-user eBook)
9781503863385 (Electronic Publication)

LCCN 2021952678

Printed in the United States of America

TABLE OF CONTENTS

Go Seahawks! 4
Becoming the Seahawks 6
By the Numbers 8
Game Day 10
Uniform 12
Team Spirit 14
Heroes of History 16
Big Days 18
Modern-Day Marvels 20
The GOAT 22
The Big Game 24
Amazing Feats 26
All-Time Best 28

    Glossary 30
    Find Out More 31
    Index and About the Author 32

GO SEAHAWKS!

The Seattle Seahawks compete in the National Football **League's** (NFL's) National Football Conference (NFC). They play in the NFC West **division**, along with the Arizona Cardinals, Los Angeles Rams, and San Francisco 49ers. Fans in Seattle have been lucky in recent years. Since 2003, the "Hawks" have only missed the **playoffs** five times. And during that same period, they've played in the **Super Bowl** three times. Let's learn more about the Seahawks!

NFC WEST DIVISION

Arizona Cardinals

Los Angeles Rams

San Francisco 49ers

Seattle Seahawks

MARSHAWN LYNCH (LEFT) AND RUSSELL WILSON (RIGHT) DROVE THE SEATTLE OFFENSE TOGETHER FOR FOUR SEASONS.

BECOMING THE SEAHAWKS

The Seahawks joined the NFL as an **expansion team** in 1976. The team was chosen after a local contest asked fans to suggest names for the team. "Seahawk" is a nickname for a bird found in the western United States called an osprey. Seattle played their first season in the NFC West division. Then they were switched to the American Football Conference (AFC) West division. Finally, they moved back to the NFC West in 2002. The Seahawks posted their first winning season in only their third year of existence when they went 9–7 in 1978.

DAVE KRIEG (RIGHT) PLAYED IN 129 GAMES AS QUARTERBACK FOR THE SEAHAWKS FROM 1980 TO 1991.

BY THE NUMBERS

The Seahawks have won **ONE** Super Bowl.

11 division titles for the Seahawks

459 points scored by the team in 2020—a Seahawks record!

13 wins for the Seahawks in 2013

QUARTERBACK MATT HASSELBECK LED THE SEAHAWKS TO THEIR FIRST-EVER APPEARANCE IN THE SUPER BOWL.

THE SEAHAWKS HAVE WON TEN PLAYOFF GAMES AT LUMEN FIELD.

GAME DAY

The Seahawks used to play their home games in the Kingdome. It was a covered **stadium** they shared with Major League Baseball's Seattle Mariners. Since 2002, their home stadium has been Lumen Field. The team shares Lumen Field with Major League Soccer's Seattle Sounders. About 69,000 fans can cheer on the Seahawks on game days. In 2013, and again in 2014, the crowd at Lumen Field set a Guinness World Record for loudest crowd noise at an outdoor stadium.

We're Famous!

Seahawks offensive lineman Dakoda Shepley might be recognized by some fans for wearing a costume instead of a uniform. Shepley appeared in the movie *Deadpool 2* as a Marvel Comics villain called Omega Red. He's a small part of the movie but has been featured heavily in comic books. In the comics, Omega Red is a super soldier with retractable metal tentacles. Pretty fierce!

UNIFORM

BLUE

WHITE

Truly Weird

Scorigami is a made-up word used to describe a score that's never before happened in the history of sports. The word is a combination of *score* and *origami*. NFL games ending in a scorigami are rare, but not for the Seahawks! From 2010 through 2018, they had a crazy streak in which they had at least one scorigami game each season! That means that at least once in each of those seasons, a game ended with a score that had never occurred in an NFL game.

Alternate Jersey

Sometimes teams wear an alternate jersey that is different from their home and away jerseys. It might be a bright color or have a unique theme. The Seahawks wore their neon green uniforms for a 2016 game. The bright uniforms proved lucky. Seattle beat the Los Angeles Rams 24–3.

FANS TAKE PRIDE IN BEING THE "12TH MAN" ON THE FIELD FOR THEIR SEAHAWKS.

TEAM SPIRIT

Going to a game at Lumen Field can be a ton of fun! The fans at the stadium have earned the nickname "The 12th Man" for their ability to impact the game. They often create so much noise that it makes it hard for the other team to communicate. And before every game, a fan or celebrity is chosen to raise The 12th Man flag in the south end zone while the crowd screams. The Seahawks Dancers are the team's cheerleading squad. They entertain the crowd at every home game. They're joined by the team's mascots. Blitz and Boom are costumed birds, and Taima is a live hawk.

BLITZ

HEROES OF HISTORY

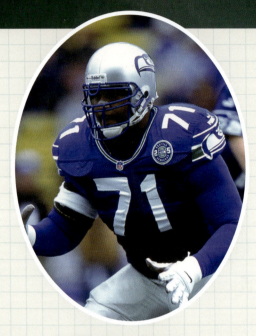

Walter Jones
Offensive Tackle | 1997–2008

Jones anchored the Seahawks' offensive line for more than a decade. He helped lead the team to its first Super Bowl appearance after the 2005 season. Jones has played in the **Pro Bowl** nine times. He's also a member of the Pro Football **Hall of Fame** and was chosen for the NFL's 100th Anniversary All-Time Team.

Cortez Kennedy
Defensive Tackle | 1990–2000

Kennedy created chaos for opposing offensive players during his 11-year career. In 1992, he finished with 14 **sacks** and was named the NFL's Defensive Player of the Year. He was chosen for the Pro Bowl eight times. In 2012, Kennedy was inducted into the Pro Football Hall of Fame.

Steve Largent
Wide Receiver | 1976–1989

Largent played 14 NFL seasons, all with the Seahawks. He is tied for ninth in NFL history with 100 **touchdown** catches. Largent led the league in receiving twice. He was chosen for the Pro Bowl seven times. Largent is a member of the Pro Football Hall of Fame and was chosen for the NFL's 100th Anniversary All-Time Team.

Legion of Boom
Cornerbacks/Safeties | 2011–2018

The "Legion of Boom" (LOB) refers to the Seahawks' dominant secondary (cornerbacks and safeties) during an era of great success for the team. Each season from 2012 to 2015, the Seahawks gave up the fewest points in the NFL. While many players contributed, three of the most important LOB members were Kam Chancellor, Richard Sherman (pictured above), and Earl Thomas.

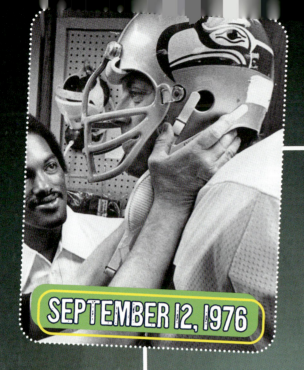

SEPTEMBER 12, 1976

The Seahawks play their first game in team history—a 30–24 loss to the St. Louis Cardinals.

The Seahawks defeat the Carolina Panthers in the NFC Championship Game, earning their first trip to the Super Bowl.

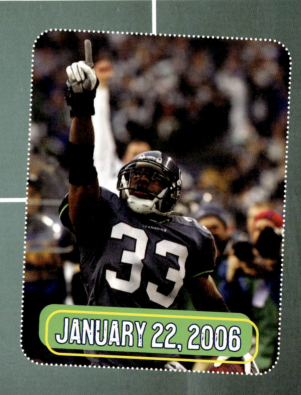

JANUARY 22, 2006

BIG DAYS

APRIL 27, 2012

With a third round selection in the NFL Draft, the Seahawks select quarterback Russell Wilson from the University of Wisconsin.

The team defeats the Green Bay Packers in the NFC Championship Game and earns its second-straight trip to the Super Bowl.

JANUARY 18, 2015

MODERN-DAY MARVELS

Jamal Adams
Safety | Debut: 2020

Adams played his first three seasons for the New York Jets. In 2020, he was traded to the Seahawks. Adams totaled 325 solo tackles and seven forced fumbles through his first five NFL seasons. He's been selected for the Pro Bowl three times.

Quandre Diggs
Safety | Debut: 2019

Diggs anchors the Seahawks' secondary. In 2020, he led the NFC with five interceptions, the most by a Seahawks player since 2015. He's started every game he's played in since joining the Seahawks. Diggs was chosen for his first Pro Bowl in 2020.

Tyler Lockett
Wide Receiver | Debut: 2015

Lockett's blazing speed makes him a dangerous wide receiver. He's gained over 1,000 yards receiving three times in his career. He's ranked in the top ten in touchdown catches three different times. He was chosen to the Pro Bowl in 2015 for his accomplishments as a punt and kick returner.

D. K. Metcalf
Wide Receiver | Debut: 2019

After he starred at the University of Mississippi, Metcalf was chosen by the Seahawks in the second round of the 2019 NFL Draft. Metcalf finished with 900 receiving yards and seven touchdown catches as a **rookie**. In 2020, he was chosen for his first Pro Bowl after finishing with 1,303 yards and ten touchdowns.

THE SEAHAWKS ONLY MISSED THE PLAYOFFS TWICE DURING WILSON'S TEN SEASONS WITH THE TEAM.

THE GOAT
GREATEST OF ALL TIME

RUSSELL WILSON

Wilson played for the Seahawks from 2012 to 2021 and led the team to a winning record nine times. He started every game from 2012 through 2020. Wilson is Seattle's career leader in passing yards (37,0590) and touchdowns (292). He led the team to 24 fourth quarter comebacks and was chosen for the Pro Bowl nine times.

FAN FAVORITE

Marshawn Lynch–Running Back
2010–2015; 2019

Lynch was known to his many fans as "Beast Mode" for his ferocious, aggressive running style. He was considered one of the toughest runners in the league to tackle. Lynch led the league in rushing touchdowns twice. He was chosen for five Pro Bowls.

THE BIG GAME

FEBRUARY 2, 2014 – SUPER BOWL 48

While the Seahawks had played in the Super Bowl once before, they had not yet won the big game. Seattle's defense ranked first in the league during the 2013 season, while the Denver Broncos' offense ranked first. Twelve seconds into the game, Seattle's defense made its presence felt when defensive end Cliff Avril tackled a Denver player in the end zone for a safety. Quarterback Russell Wilson threw two touchdown passes. Linebacker Malcolm Smith was named the game's **Most Valuable Player** for a 69-yard interception return touchdown. The Seahawks won their first Super Bowl ever, 43–8.

WIDE RECEIVER JERMAINE KEARSE SCORED A TOUCHDOWN IN THE THIRD QUARTER OF SUPER BOWL 48.

PETE CARROLL HAS LED THE SEAHAWKS TO TEN PLAYOFF VICTORIES, INCLUDING ONE SUPER BOWL TITLE.

AMAZING FEATS

40 Touchdown Passes — In 2020 by **QUARTERBACK** Russell Wilson

27 Rushing Touchdowns — In 2005 by **RUNNING BACK** Shaun Alexander

14 Touchdown Catches — In 2015 by **WIDE RECEIVER** Doug Baldwin

16.5 Sacks — In 1998 by **DEFENSIVE END** Michael Sinclair

ALL-TIME BEST

PASSING YARDS
Russell Wilson
37,059
Matt Hasselbeck
29,434
Dave Krieg
26,132

RUSHING YARDS
Shaun Alexander
9,429
Chris Warren
6,706
Curt Warner
6,705

RECEIVING YARDS
Steve Largent
13,089
Brian Blades
7,620
Doug Baldwin
6,563

SACKS*
Jacob Green
115.5
Michael Sinclair
73.5
Jeff Bryant
63

SCORING
Norm Johnson
810
Stephen Hauschka
759
Shaun Alexander
672

INTERCEPTIONS
Dave Brown
50
Eugene Robinson
42
John Harris
41

*unofficial before 1982

SHAUN ALEXANDER'S 27 RUSHING TOUCHDOWNS IN 2005 ARE TIED FOR THE SECOND-MOST EVER IN A SINGLE SEASON.

GLOSSARY

division (dih-VIZSH-un): a group of teams within the NFL who play each other more frequently and compete for the best record

expansion team (ek-SPAN-shun TEEM): a new team added to the league

Hall of Fame (HAHL of FAYM): a museum in Canton, Ohio, that honors the best players in NFL history

league (LEEG): an organization of sports teams that compete against each other

Most Valuable Player (MOHST VALL-yuh-bul PLAY-uhr): a yearly award given to the top player in the NFL

playoffs (PLAY-ahfs): a series of games after the regular season that decides which two teams play in the Super Bowl

Pro Bowl (PRO BOWL): the NFL's All-Star game where the best players in the league compete

rookie (RUH-kee): a player playing in his first season

sack (SAK): when a quarterback is tackled behind the line of scrimmage before he can throw the ball

stadium (STAY-dee-uhm): a building with a field and seats for fans where teams play

Super Bowl (SOO-puhr BOWL): the championship game of the NFL, played between the winners of the AFC and the NFC

touchdown (TUTCH-down): a play in which the ball is brought into the other team's end zone, resulting in six points

FIND OUT MORE

IN THE LIBRARY

Bulgar, Beth and Mark Bechtel. *My First Book of Football*.
New York, NY: Time Inc. Books, 2015.

Jacobs, Greg. *The Everything Kids' Football Book, 7th Edition*.
Avon, MA: Adams Media, 2021.

Sports Illustrated Kids. *The Greatest Football Teams of All Time*.
New York, NY: Time Inc. Books, 2018.

Temple, Ramey. Seattle Seahawks. New York, NY: AV2, 2020.

ON THE WEB

Visit our website for links about the Seattle Seahawks:
childsworld.com/links

Note to parents, teachers, and librarians: We routinely verify our web links to make sure they are safe and active sites. Encourage your readers to check them out!

INDEX

Avril, Cliff 24

Blitz 15
Boom 15

Carroll, Pete 26
Chancellor, Cam 17

Diggs, Quandre 20

Jones, Walter 16

Kennedy, Cortez 16
Kingdome 11

Largent, Steve 17, 28
Legion of Boom 17
Lockett, Tyler 21
Lumen Field 10–11, 15
Lynch, Marshawn 5, 23

Metcalf, D. K. 21

National Football Conference (NFC) 4, 7, 18–20
NFL Draft 19, 21

Shepley, Dakoda 11
Sherman, Richard 17
Smith, Malcolm 24
Super Bowl 4, 8–9, 16, 18–19, 24–26

Taima 15
The 12th Man 14–15
Thomas, Earl 17

Wilson, Russell 5, 19, 22–24, 27–28

ABOUT THE AUTHOR

Josh Anderson has published over 50 books for children and young adults. His two boys are the greatest joys in his life. Hobbies include coaching his sons in youth basketball, no-holds-barred games of Apples to Apples, and taking long family walks. His favorite NFL team is a secret he'll never share!